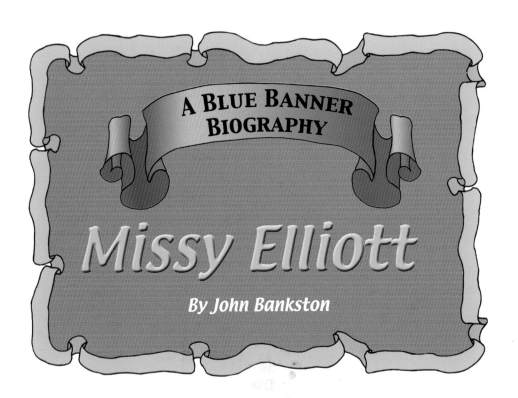

A BLUE BANNER BIOGRAPHY

Missy Elliott

By John Bankston

P.O. Box 196
Hockessin, Delaware 19707
Visit us on the web: www.mitchelllane.com
Comments? email us: mitchelllane@mitchelllane.com

Printing   2   3   4   5   6   7   8   9

Blue Banner Biographies

Alicia Keys	Allen Iverson	Avril Lavigne
Beyoncé	Bow Wow	Britney Spears
Christina Aguilera	Christopher Paul Curtis	Clay Aiken
Condoleezza Rice	Daniel Radcliffe	Derek Jeter
Eminem	Eve	Ja Rule
Jay-Z	Jennifer Lopez	J.K. Rowling
Jodie Foster	Lance Armstrong	Mary-Kate and Ashley Olsen
Melissa Gilbert	Michael Jackson	**Missy Elliott**
Nelly	P. Diddy	Queen Latifah
Rita Williams-Garcia	Ritchie Valens	Ron Howard
Rudy Giuliani	Sally Field	Selena
Shirley Temple		

Library of Congress Cataloging-in-Publication Data
Bankston, John, 1974-
        Missy Elliott / John Bankston.
                p. cm. — (A blue banner biography)
Includes bibliographical references (p.   ) and index.
Discography: p.
Contents: Discovery — Sista — Behind the music — Combs and Misdemeanor — Breaking the cycle.
        ISBN 1-58415-219-2 (library bound)
    1. Elliott, Missy—Juvenile literature. 2. Singers—United States—Biography—Juvenile litera-
    ture. [1. Elliott, Missy. 2. Singers. 3. African Americans—Biography. 4. Women—Biography.] I.
    Title. II. Series.
        ML3930.E45 B3 2003
        782.421649'092--dc22
                                                                                    2003024037

ABOUT THE AUTHOR: Born in Boston, Massachussetts, **John Bankston** began publishing articles in newspapers and magazines while still a teenager. Since then, he has written over two hundred articles, and contributed chapters to books such as *Crimes of Passion,* and *Death Row 2000,* which have been sold in bookstores across the world. He has written numerous biographies for young adults, including *Eminem* and *Nelly* (Mitchell Lane). He currently lives in Portland, Oregon.
PHOTO CREDITS: Cover: Getty Images; p. 4 Getty Images; p. 12 Albert L. Ortega/WireImage; p. 14 Michael Caulfield/WireImage; p. 16 Dave Allocca/DMI/Time Life Pictures/Getty Images; p. 20 Corbis Sygma; p. 22 AP Photo/The Daily Press, Joe Fudge; p. 24 Kevin Mazur/WireImage; p. 25 Reuters NewMedia, Inc./Corbis; p. 27 Theo Wargo/WireImage
ACKNOWLEDGMENTS: The following story has been thoroughly researched, and to the best of our knowledge, represents a true story. While every possible effort has been made to ensure accuracy, the publisher will not assume liability for damages caused by inaccuracies in the data, and makes no warranty on the accuracy of the information contained herein. This story has not been authorized nor endorsed by Missy Elliott.

CONTENTS

Missy Elliott's innovative style got her an audition with Devante of Jodeci. Today her style and uniqueness are key to her endurance as a top hip-hop artist.

Discovery

Missy Elliott was nervous. As she and her three friends approached the hotel room, she wasn't sure what to expect. They'd just watched the popular band Jodeci perform. The group of young women had dressed up for the event, wearing outfits their mothers bought for them. They'd even managed to get back-stage passes. Unfortunately, after the show, the person they were looking for, Devante Swing, the charismatic songwriter who performed with the group, wasn't around.

Now they hoped to find him in his room.

They weren't fans or groupies. They were singers, part of a group called Sista. Missy was their leader. She'd auditioned the other singers; she'd written most of their songs. She'd even convinced them to dress like Jodeci, imitating their style, with jeans tucked in their boots and distinctive canes. "We thought we were four hot Devantes," Missy admitted.

The gimmick worked. When they met Devante in his room, he was intrigued enough by their clothes and Missy's confidence to let them sing. "I had won talent shows and all that, but this was gonna be a real audition," Missy continued. "I made sure we had all original music." The four women sang their best, and Devante quickly realized they could be the perfect opening act for Jodeci. He told the women he'd fly them to New York to his record label's headquarters.

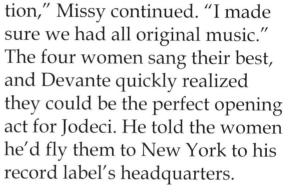

Missy and her group Sista met Jodeci's Devante. He was intrigued enough to let them audition.

Missy was 19 years old, and she knew she was on her way.

Melissa Elliott was born July 1, 1972, in Portsmouth, Virginia. The little girl, nicknamed Missy by her mother, Patricia, grew up an only child. Sometimes that made her home life even harder to bear. Without any brothers or sisters, it seemed like she was stuck between her parents, who were always fighting.

Music was her escape. Most little kids like to sing to themselves or play on makeshift instruments. To Missy, these games were important. She'd sing silly songs to cheer herself up or personal songs about what was happening in her home. She never stopped singing.

"When I was five, I was making up stupid little songs . . . ," she later told *Billboard* magazine. "I used to stand outside on top of a garbage can, holding my little broom, and just sing about butterflies or whatever."

In many ways she was just a kid with an active imagination. She'd sing to her dolls and then make them clap at the end of her "performance." She'd watch TV shows like *American Bandstand* and pretend she was up on stage, singing to the group of dancing teens or being interviewed by host Dick Clark.

The singing games became more valuable as she got older and her parents' fighting intensified. According to Missy, her father began hitting her mother. The young girl would hide out in her room, turning up the radio or scribbling down lyrics.

Sometimes her room wasn't far enough away. When she was 11, her mother and father got into a terrifying argument. Although her dad had hit her mother before, this time seemed even worse. Missy was afraid her father was going to kill Patricia or that he might come after her. Missy fled the house. She didn't worry that it was snowing. She didn't even bother with shoes. As she recalled, she made the way two miles to her aunt's house, where she was safe.

> *As Missy's parents' fighting intensified, Missy hid out in her room, turning up the radio or scribbling down lyrics.*

It took almost two more years before Patricia had enough courage to leave her husband. By the time Missy was 13, her mother had had enough. She took her daughter and left. "My mother leaving my father changed my life," Missy told *Ebony.* "It made me a stronger person. Just watching her and picking up her ways."

Although the separation ended the fighting, not everything got better. Money was tight, and Patricia worked long hours as a dispatcher at the local power company. Once Missy skipped lunch for weeks, saving the money to buy her mom a pair of red shoes she'd admired.

> *Once Missy skipped lunch for weeks to buy her mom a pair of red shoes she'd admired.*

As an only child, Missy spent a lot of time alone, time she used writing songs and picking up on the latest music. The songs she wrote were poems really; she imagined the music in her head.

On the radio it seemed like the closest thing to what she was writing was hip-hop, which in the early 1980s was just becoming popular. Groups like Run DMC and the Beastie Boys were getting radio play and being featured on MTV. Although Missy loved the music, judging by the videos she saw on MTV, there didn't seem to be a place for her in hip-hop. The only women she saw in videos weren't singers, they were models, barely better than set decorations, and no more important than the plants or the floats in the pool.

In 1988 a group named Salt-N-Pepa changed all that. The three young African-American women proved they could be as successful as male hip-hop stars as they rapped about their own experiences. Their anthem "Push It" became a hit song.

Missy was mesmerized. Suddenly there was a group of women in hip-hop that were more than just set decorations. "They were some of the first women to stick with it in rap," she explained on Elektra.com.

After hearing their song, Missy became more focused. She put everything she had into music. Although she'd been singing in the church choir with her mother for years, she began to enter talent shows. Sometimes she'd get a group of friends to enter with her. Missy allowed herself to imagine a future in which she used her voice to rap about the life she knew and the issues she'd faced as a child.

The all-female group Salt-N-Pepa proved that women could be as successful as men in hip-hop.

In 1990 she graduated from high school. She decided to stop dreaming and start doing. She wasn't going to college. Instead Missy hoped to get her education in the music industry. She had no idea what a difficult school the school of hip-hop was going to be.

Sista

*T*ests Missy Elliott had taken in school proved she was smart. An IQ test put her in the gifted range. Despite the exams, her grades in high school were poor. She often failed her classes and barely managed to graduate. "When I got home from school, I wasn't thinking about homework," she told *Ebony*. "I was thinking about putting on a Michael Jackson record and getting in the mirror and imitating him."

Yet she quickly demonstrated her intelligence when she began pursuing a music career. For one thing, Missy decided not to do it alone. Instead of being a solo singer, Missy was going to start a "girl group." So called for their all-female members, girl groups have been consistent chart toppers since 1958's The Chantals. Some have been just singers, like the Spice Girls or En Vogue; others also played instruments, like the Go-Gos or Sleater-Kinney. From harmonizers Diana Ross and the Supremes of the 1960s, to the 1970s' teen rockers the Runaways and the 1980s' Southern California punk-influenced Go-Gos, to today's Dixie Chicks and Destiny's Child, girl groups have one thing in common: they get attention partly because they're female. No one writes a gender-related article about all-male groups, but even in the new millennium, members of girl groups get press partly because of their gender.

Even worse, many all-female bands are assembled by men. Men audition young women who don't know each other and turn them into groups like the Spice Girls or En Vogue. The women's looks often seem more important than their musical ability.

Missy Elliott didn't want that. She realized she didn't look like most of the women in the girl groups—she was heavier, for one thing—but even if she did, she didn't want a record deal based on appearance. "I'm not a follower," she told *Ebony*. "I'm not a copycat. I'm an original. That's important to staying around for a long time."

Missy realized there were girl groups that kept turning out hits, and others that fell apart after one

Even though an IQ test placed Missy in the gifted range, her grades in high school were poor.

album. She figured part of the reason Salt-N-Pepa had staying power was because they weren't relying on their looks to keep an audience interested. Missy decided looks fade, skills endure, and her girl group was going to be based on talent over everything else.

When she decided to form a group, she enlisted the help of Tim "Timbaland" Mosley, a fellow Virginian she'd met a few years before. She would do the songwriting, he'd do the producing, and the pair would work together to find a group of women with a unique sound. They also decided to create original music and rely less on samples — the popular technique in hip-hop of taking parts of an existing song and remixing them.

Missy is shown here with Tweet (left) and Timbaland (right) holding a Soul Train award. Missy and Timbaland have worked together as songwriter and producer since Missy put together her girl group Sista.

After a series of auditions, Missy found the women she wanted to work with, and Sista was formed. The four women began making the rounds of talent shows and open mic nights at local clubs in Virginia, trying to get noticed. Missy refused to rely on luck. When she learned that Jodeci was coming to Portsmouth, she planned to be at their show.

Although the group was made up of two sets of brothers (Joel and Cedric Hailey and Dalvin and Donald DeGrate), Jodeci's main producer and songwriter was Donald DeGrate, who went by the stage name Devante Swing. The group was signed to Uptown Records, a division of Elektra. Success came early. Their debut album sold two million copies. Devante Swing was given the chance to find and develop new talent. For Missy, that was the best reason to make sure she met him when he came through Virginia.

> *Although Missy's group was performing in talent shows and open mic nights at clubs, Missy refused to rely on luck.*

After Sista's audition, Devante had an easy time picturing Sista opening for Jodeci on tour. He gave them a shot. A few days later, Missy and the rest of her group flew to New York and signed a deal with Jodeci's label.

In 1991, Sista began opening for Jodeci and released a single, "Brand New." That was as close as they got.

Financial problems at Uptown kept their debut album from ever being released. By the middle 1990s, Sista had broken up.

Missy was disappointed by Sista's failure, but the breakup presented her with new opportunities. Devante recognized her songwriting skills and decided to give her and Timbaland another break.

Missy could make a living doing what she'd started doing as a kid. Not singing songs. *Writing* them.

Early in Missy's music career, she wasn't performing the songs, she was writing them. Today, her success in songwriting has allowed her to do both.

Behind the Music

*P*utting together an album is hard work — long hours in the studio crafting the perfect sound, meetings with producers and record executives, not to mention the labor of writing or at least selecting the best songs. The whole process can take months, even years. So when all of Sista's hard work resulted in an album that didn't even get released, Missy was upset. But she wasn't about to give up.

"I never wanted to do anything else but music. I felt I had a God-given talent and I'd get in some way," she later told *The New York Times.* Jodeci's Devante Swing believed Missy and her collaborator Timbaland were the best things about Sista — he knew they'd done most of the songwriting and producing on the group's debut. He offered to move the pair into a house in Hackensack, New Jersey, (not far from New York City) and put them to work creating songs for other artists.

It was the perfect opportunity.

The music business is similar to the rest of the entertainment industry. Stars get all the attention. They get the fans, the magazine covers, the videos. But in many cases it's the behind-the-scenes players who have the long careers and wind up making the most money. In music, both singers and songwriters are paid royalties, a small percentage of each album sold. Although this can mean literally millions of dollars for some top stars,

Missy is shown here in 1999 with Aaliyah (left) and rapper Nas (center). Missy and Timbaland began writing and producing songs for Aaliyah after she and producer R. Kelly went separate ways.

most singers have to pay back the record label for studio time, concert tours, and video-production expenses. Songwriters don't have these types of costs, so often the person who writes the song brings home more money than the person who sings it.

As Missy later admitted to *Newsweek*, "I love songwriting and producing because it's where I make my real money."

In the beginning, Missy and Timbaland wrote and produced songs for Jodeci and Ginuwine, who'd signed a deal with Elektra the same day as Sista. However, it was Missy's work with other young women that got the executives at her label talking.

Teen star Aaliyah had a falling out with her producer R. Kelly, and Elektra executive Craig Clavin asked Missy and Timbaland to take over work on her album. The songs the pair wrote and produced became hits for the young star and convinced another up-and-coming music producer, Sean "P. Diddy" Combs, to enlist Missy for a remix of Gina Thompson's "The Things You Do."

Not only did Missy help with the remix, she added her own voice to the recording. Her distinctive laugh

> *Because most singers have to pay the record label for expenses, the person who writes the song usually brings home more money.*

didn't just earn Missy a new nickname, the Hee Ha Girl. It earned her her own label.

Sylvia Rhone was the head of Elektra when Missy was getting listed as songwriter on dozens of songs. As Rhone is quoted, "In this fiercely competitive business, you have to earn respect." Missy had worked hard and earned it, and by 1995 Rhone said, "You could instantly recognize that Missy possessed star potential."

Rhone gave Missy the chance to run her own label. GoldMind Records would not only give her the opportunity to write and produce, but also to discover new talent. Missy Elliott's first discovery was Missy Elliott.

GoldMind Records gave Missy the opportunity to write, produce, and discover new talent.

Combs and Misdemeanor

*I*n 1997, Sean Combs moved from being a behind-the-scenes producer to an onstage performer. He was motivated partly by creative drive but also by the murder of his close friend Christopher "Notorious B.I.G." Wallace. Combs's remix of the Police hit "Every Breath You Take" was a musical eulogy, sung in memory of his dear friend. As he worked on his own album, Combs also encouraged fellow producer Missy Elliott to return to performing.

He wasn't alone. Friends and fellow record executives at Elektra often asked Missy when she was going to step back in front of the mic. Missy wasn't afraid of the spotlight, she was afraid of not having anything to say. In late 1996, she realized she had something to offer.

"I took a look around," Missy recalled. "I realized we went through years of 'I hate you' records, and then

Shown here in this 1997 picture, Missy grabbed listeners' attentions with flashy outfits and inventive videos.

we went through 'Gimme my money' records." If Missy's ideas for her album could be put into a phrase, it might be, "I want to be with you, but you've got some problems."

"Most relationships are not a beautiful picture," she admitted to *Rolling Stone* magazine. "I try to capture the real side of things." Besides presenting her unique point of view, Missy also added artists she'd written songs for, like Busta Rhymes, Aaliyah, and Ginuwine, who contributed to her album's 16 tracks.

According to Missy, she completed her own work on the album in a week. It was an amazing accomplishment, but not for someone who says she and Timbaland rarely spend more than half an hour on any one song. By the time she began working on *Supa Dupa Fly*, her debut album, she and Timbaland had abandoned the New York music scene for Virginia and a Virginia Beach recording studio. "I think that studio gives us a home feeling," she explained in a July 1999 *The Music Monitor* article. "It's a very small studio, about the size of a bedroom."

Her debut was helped by an inventive and fun video in which Missy avoided the standard hip-hop clichés by bouncing around in a shiny outfit that made her look like a puffy alien. "I'm very futuristic in my thinking, my imagining and the kind of music I make. It fits my style," she explained to *Automotive News*.

Supa really was super, rocketing to number three on the *Billboard* album chart the first week of its release. Besides appealing to fans of hip-hop, the CD crossed over, reaching pop and rock listeners as well.

As a songwriter, Missy was well known in the record industry, but in 1997 she became known to record buyers as Missy "Misdemeanor" Elliott. "I'm still Missy . . . ," she explained to *The Music Monitor*.

> *Besides appealing to hip-hop fans, Missy's debut album crossed over to reach pop and rock listeners as well.*

"When I go home and deal with people like my aunts and uncles, they still treat me like Missy." Her fans, however, wanted Misdemeanor, and they begged for live performances. Although she appeared at the Lilith Fair, a music festival that featured predominantly white, female folk singers, Missy was uncomfortable with the idea of a full-fledged tour.

"She's a studio rat," Elektra head Rhone told *Rolling Stone.* "She lives in the studio. She's not a big social person. Her home is her music, her safe place is her music. That's the way she rolls."

Yet as a new millennium approached, Missy would come out of her safe place, first to talk about the past, and then to mourn a friend.

Missy is shown here performing at the Lilith Fair. She is more comfortable recording in the studio than making live appearances.

Breaking the Cycle

Missy Elliott had been working in the music business since she was a teenager. In many ways she was better prepared for the success of her solo debut than other young hip-hop stars. In fact, her unique musical style helped others as much as it helped her.

"Missy has developed into one of contemporary music's most original stars, without succumbing to negative stereotypes or sexual clichés," explained Elektra's chairman Sylvia Rhone. "She's opened many doors for other African-American artists and executives."

Missy's new star power didn't just help those trying to break into the music business. Because of her honesty, she was able to help many young women struggling with the aftermath of abuse. Not long after her first album came out, Missy began discussing the truth of her childhood. She spoke about being molested by an older cousin and about her father's violence. No one was more surprised by this than her mother.

"Initially I was stunned," Patricia Elliott admitted, according to mme.330.ca. "There was a lot of hurt and turmoil in our past that I'd put in the closet so no one

Although Missy's songs are creative and lighthearted, she spoke out about the serious issues of domestic violence and sexual abuse. She hoped her openness about her experiences would help listeners who were in similar situations.

In 2003, Missy received an MTV Video Music Award for Best Video. She was given the award for her video "Work It."

would really know." Missy's mom supported her daughter's courage in speaking out. Missy's work with the domestic violence organization Break the Cycle helped many of her listeners who'd either survived domestic violence or who were living in households affected by it.

The late 1990s weren't all about issues for Missy. She was nominated for three MTV Video Music Awards for her first video and three Grammy Awards. Although it would take her several years to win a

Grammy (she won one in 2002 and one in 2003), she was nominated for many music awards before then.

In 1999, Missy released her second album, *Da Real World*. At first it wasn't as successful as her debut, and many in the industry wondered if she'd suffered the notorious sophomore slump. Maybe listeners were put off by its first single, which had a title using a negative word for a woman. "Because a lot of females are aggressive and in control of their destiny, they get called that a lot of time," Missy told *Billboard* magazine. "After hearing the record and how I'm using it, I think people got past the word."

Despite all the good things happening for Missy, in 2001 her friend and fellow artist Aaliyah died in a plane crash.

Maybe, maybe not, but it was the album's third single, "Hot Boyz," which sold over one million copies, stayed at number one on the rap single charts for 18 weeks (a new record), and pushed *Da Real World* into multi-million-seller status.

The rapper who said she was singing for the year 2000 celebrated the new millennium considerably thinner and in more demand than ever as a producer. She also did commercials for a soft drink, and from her third album, *Miss E . . . So Addictive,* "One Minute Man" became a club favorite.

Missy is shown here filming the video for Aaliyah's "Miss You." The video, which was filmed as a tribute to the late Aaliyah, features many artists remembering Aaliyah and lip synching the words to her song.

Despite all the good news, tragedy again touched Missy's life. Just a short time before the nation's mourning of September 11, 2001, Missy mourned the loss of singer Aaliyah, with whom she'd collaborated for years. After Aaliyah's death in a plane crash, Missy would join TLC in a duet. Featured on 2002's album *Under Construction*, their song would celebrate the lives of Aaliyah and TLC's Lisa "Left Eye" Lopez, who had died in a car crash.

In November 2003, Missy released her fifth album, *This is Not a Test.* The album demonstrated her talent and included artists such as Jay-Z, Monica and Timbaland. 2003 had already been a good year for Missy, having won her second Grammy and receiving a standing ovation at the American Music Awards. She also starred in a Gap commercial with Madonna and took home the highest honor at the MTV Video Music Awards for her video "Work It."

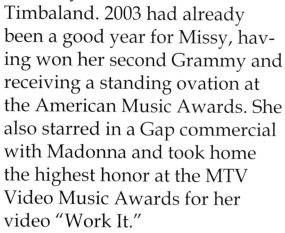

Missy filmed her video "Gossip Folks" in a high school and played one of the students.

In 2003, Missy also returned to a place of pain with humor and power. She decided to film her video "Gossip Folks" in a high school and play one of the kids. As she explained to *In Style* magazine, "I'm sort of an outcast and everyone is whispering and picking on me. But by the end I'm the boss of the school." For Missy it was a familiar feeling, going from an only child who felt on the outside to the boss running her own successful label and looking toward the future.

CHRONOLOGY

1972   Melissa Elliott is born on July 1 in Portsmouth, Virginia

1985   Missy's parents separate; she stays with her mother

1990   After graduating from high school, she forms the group Sista

1991   Sista is signed to a record deal with Elektra Entertainment

1993   After Sista's debut album is not released, Missy begins working as a songwriter

1995   GoldMind, Missy's own record label, is formed as a division of Elektra

1996   Writes songs for Aaliyah's album

1997   Debut album, *Supa Dupa Fly*, reaches No. 3 on the *Billboard* charts in its first week

1998   Becomes one of first hip-hop artists to join the all-female Lilith Fair

1999   Misdemeanor lipstick is introduced; some of its sales will benefit the organization Break the Cycle

2001   Aaliyah is killed in a plane crash

2003   Appears in ad for the Gap with Madonna; *This Is Not a Test,* featuring "Pass That Dutch," is released

FOR FURTHER READING

Chappell, Kevin. "Eve and Missy Elliott: Taking Rap to a New Level." *Ebony,* August 2001, p. 68ff.

Chambers, Veronica. "Be Like Mike?" *Newsweek,* October 6, 1997, p. 77.

Lee, Elyssa. "Schoolhouse Rap." *In Style,* March 2003, p. 294.

Nelson, Havelock. *Billboard,* June 21, 1997.

Silberger, K. "Super Fly Girl: Missy Elliott Bugs Out." *Rolling Stone,* October 2, 1997, p. 22.

On the Web:

Missy Misdemeanor Elliott: First Biography
  http://mme.330.ca/firstbiography.html

BBC: Missy Elliott
  http://www.bbc.co.uk/music/profiles/elliotmissy.shtml

Elektra: Missy Elliott Homepage
  http://www.elektra.com/elektra/missyelliott/index.jhtml

Da World According to Missy
  http://www.penduluminc.com/MM/july99/missyelliot.html

Rock on the Net: Missy Elliott
  http://www.rockonthenet.com/artists-e/missyelliott_main.htm

MTV.com: Missy Elliott
  http://www.mtv.com/bands/az/elliott_missy/artist.jhtml

The Official Missy Elliott Site
  http://www.missy-elliott.com

DISCOGRAPHY

1997 *Supa Dupa Fly*
1999 *Da Real World*
2001 *Miss E . . . So Addictive*
2002 *Under Construction*
2003 *This Is Not a Test*

SELECTED AWARDS

1997 Two Billboard Video Music Awards
2000 Soul Train Lady of Soul Award for Best R&B or Rap Video
2001 Soul Train Lady of Soul Award for Best R&B or Rap Video
2002 Soul Train Award for R&B/Soul or Rap Music Video
Grammy Award for Best Rap Solo Performance
BET Award for Best Female Hip-Hop Artist
Soul Train Lady of Soul Award for Best R&B/Soul or Rap
   Music Video
2003 Grammy Award for Best Female Rap Solo Performance
MTV Video Music Award for Video of the Year
Soul Train Music Award for Best R&B/Soul or Rap Music
   Video
BET Award for Best Female Hip-Hop Artist
Soul Train Lady of Soul Awards for Best Song and Best
   Music Video
American Music Award for Favorite Rap/Hip-Hop Female
   Artist
Vibe Award for Reelest Video

INDEX